WAYNE ROONEY

UNAUTHORISED BIOGRAPHY

John Townsend

www.raintreepublishers.co.uk
Visit our website to find out more information about Raintree books.

To order:
☎ Phone 44 (0) 1865 888112
🖹 Send a fax to 44 (0) 1865 314091
💻 Visit the Raintree bookshop at www.raintreepublishers.co.uk to browse our catalogue and order online.

Raintree is an imprint of Pearson Education Limited, a company incorporated in England and Wales having its registered office at Edinburgh Gate, Harlow, Essex, CM20 2JE – Registered company number: 00872828

Raintree is a registered trademark of Pearson Education Limited

Editorial: Catherine Veitch
Design: Richard Parker and Q2A Solutions
Illustrations: Oxford Designers and Illustrators
Picture research: Mica Brancic
Production: Victoria Fitzgerald

Originated by Dot Gradations Ltd
Printed in China by CTPS

ISBN 978 1 4062 0951 8
12 11 10 09 08
10 9 8 7 6 5 4 3 2 1

British Library Cataloguing in Publication Data
Townsend, John
Wayne Rooney. – (Sport files)
796.3'34'092
A full catalogue record for this book is available from the British Library.

Acknowledgements
We would like to thank the following for permission to reproduce photographs: © Action Images (Darren Walsh Livepic) p. 5; © All Action Pictures Ltd (Claude Haller) p. 10; © AP Photo (Jon Super) p. 21; © Corbis pp. 13 (Simon Bellis), 15 (Photomorgana), 19 (Reuters/Simon Bellis), 26 (epa/Sergei Ilnitsky), 27 (Reuters/Mike Finn-Kelcey); © Eamonn and James Clarke (EMPICS Entertainment/PA Photos) p. 20; © Getty Images pp. 9 (Alex Livesey), 14 (Laurence Griffiths), 16 (AFP/Adrian Dennis), 17 (AFP Photo/Patrik Stollarz), 23 (Stuart Wilson); © Matthew Ashton (AMA/Corbis) p. 6; © NI Syndication (The Times/Marc Aspland) p. 25; © PA Archive (PA Photos) p. 24; © Rex Features (Paul Webb) p. 7.

Cover photograph of Wayne Rooney reproduced with permission of ©Getty Images (Shaun Botterill).

Every effort has been made to contact copyright holders of material reproduced in this book. Any omissions will be rectified in subsequent printings if notice is given to the publishers.

CONTENTS

Some words are printed in bold, **like this.** You can find out what they mean by looking in the glossary.

How many boys dream of playing football for their country before they are 18? It can't really happen – or can it? In 2003 that dream came true for one boy: Wayne Rooney. At the age of 17, he even scored for England! Wayne became an instant hero. In fact, he was the youngest person ever to score for England.

Wayne's other dream had already come true a few months earlier when he won the BBC Young Sports Personality of the Year. His name soon became known around the country and all his years of training were finally paying off. People were already saying he would be the next sporting superstar, and that is exactly what happened.

FAST FACT FILE

Name:	Wayne Rooney
Born:	24 October 1985, Croxteth, Liverpool
Height:	1.78 m (5 ft 10 in)
Weight:	78 kg (172 lbs)
Family:	Mum Jeanette, dad Thomas, brothers Graham and John
Position:	Forward
Preferred foot:	Right
Premier League Debut:	Everton 17/08/2002 (v Tottenham)
Professional career:	Everton: 17/01/2003 to 31/08/2004 England: 12/02/2003 Manchester United: 31/08/2004
Shirt numbers:	10 (Manchester United), 9 (England)

Teenage star

The **media** began watching Wayne Rooney with great interest. This bright new football star brought skill, talent, and excitement to the game. The crowds loved to watch him play. Newspapers wrote stories about him. Football managers kept a close eye on him, too. When Wayne was only 18 years old, Manchester United paid a fee for him that could reach up to £30 million. That's more than anyone had ever paid for a teenage footballer before.

After watching Wayne play, football manager Steve Bruce said, "I don't think any of us have seen anything like that from an 18-year-old before. Wayne is just an incredible talent. What amazes you about him is he just looks like he is going for a kick-about in the park."

Wayne Rooney is sometimes called "Roonaldo" after the Brazilian star Ronaldo.

It's not a surprise that Wayne grew up to love football. His parents were great football fans and Wayne kicked a ball as soon as he could walk. He grew up in a small house in Croxteth in Liverpool. He watched football matches on television and like his parents, Thomas and Jeanette, he became a keen supporter of Everton, the local football team.

Like other children, Wayne filled his bedroom with Everton pictures and posters. His two younger brothers – Graham (born 1987) and John (born 1990) – also became keen Everton fans. Their parents took them to local matches and it wasn't long before Wayne decided that he wanted to become a footballer.

Wayne and his brothers played football in the streets around their home. It was soon clear he had a special skill with the ball. By the age of seven he was scoring goals for a local schoolboys' team. As a member of the Liverpool Schools Under-11 side, Wayne scored a total of 72 goals and broke the team's scoring record. Their coach said about Wayne: "He had such ability. He just went ahead and did his thing."

Everton's home ground is called Goodison Park. Wayne often went there to watch matches.

The next big step

A **talent scout** from Everton Football Club spotted Wayne when he was just nine years old. He was invited along to the club's famous ground at Goodison Park and offered a place at Everton's Youth **Academy.** Here he was able to improve his skills at the very place he dreamed about. He couldn't have wished for a better offer!

Wayne's father, mother, and brother cheer him on at the Euro 2004 England v Portugal match.

As a forward, Wayne impressed the staff at the Everton **Academy** with his goal scoring, his passing ability, and his speed on the pitch. He attended the football academy after school and at weekends, and he improved all the time. When he was 12 years old, Wayne was thrilled to be chosen as the Everton **mascot** at a big match in front of a huge crowd. Now he knew what it was like to stand in the middle of the pitch in front of the cheering fans – and he loved it.

Nothing but the best

Wayne was doing so well that by the time he was 15, he was already playing for the Under-19s side. As a member of the Everton Youth Team, Wayne scored eight goals in eight matches and reached the 2002 Youth Cup Final. Wayne was already well known at Everton and before long many more people had heard of him. After another year, while still in the youth team, he made his football **Premier League debut** in August 2002 against Tottenham. At just 16 years old, he ran on to the pitch in the blue kit of Everton to the roar of the crowd. Wayne could hardly believe his dream had come true.

WHAT IS A FOOTBALL ACADEMY?

An academy is a special training centre set up by football clubs to develop young players. Most Premier League clubs have them.

The Everton Youth Academy is a football training school. Talented young players are taught football skills here, hoping to become professional footballers one day. Between the ages of 6 and 16, these young players attend normal school during the day and are coached three times a week in the evenings before taking part in Sunday matches. When they leave school, they may be offered a **scholarship** for a further three years.

Did you know?

Everton's **motto** is "*Nil Satis Nisi Optimum*", which means "Nothing but the best is good enough."

Wayne Rooney was determined to become just that – the very best.

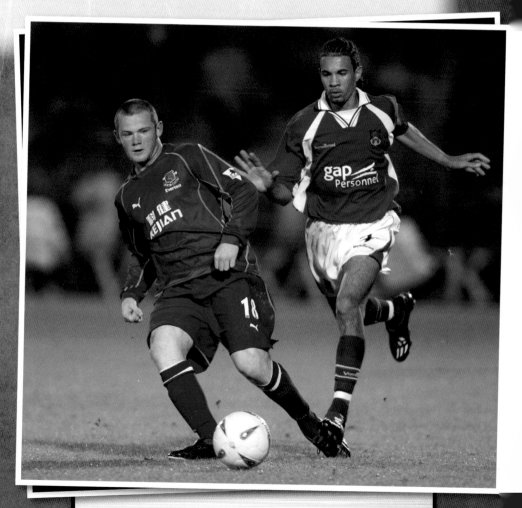

Wayne once wore a T-shirt reading: "Once a blue, always a blue." He didn't keep to this rule!

16 years old, Wayne Rooney was still too young to become a full **professional** ...yer at Everton. He was still living with his parents and playing in the youth team ... £80 a week. But on 19 October 2002, just a few days before his 17th birthday, ...yne made history. He scored just a few minutes after being brought on as a ...bstitute in an important match against Arsenal. He kicked the ball into the net ...d scored the winning goal for Everton. The crowd went wild as Everton won 2-1. ...s 2002 goal against Arsenal made Wayne Rooney the youngest Everton goalscorer, ...well as the youngest player at that time to score in the history of **Premier League** ...otball – an achievement he took over from Michael Owen.

...er such an outstanding performance Wayne became famous. Everyone in football ...d beyond knew the name of Wayne Rooney.

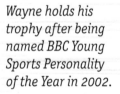

Wayne holds his trophy after being named BBC Young Sports Personality of the Year in 2002.

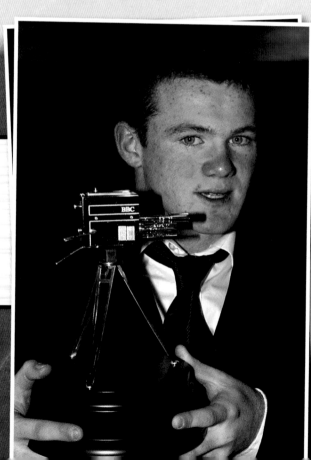

Some of Wayne's records have since been broken. James Vaughan became the youngest ever Premier League goalscorer when he scored for Everton against Crystal Palace in 2005. He was 16 years and 271 days old, breaking the previous record set by James Milner (16 years and 357 days old).

Another big year

In 2003 Wayne became a fully signed-up professional player for Everton. This meant he could also be selected to play for the England team. It didn't take long for the England manager to choose the 17-year-old to play for the national team.

CAN YOU BELIEVE IT?

- Wayne became the England team's youngest ever professional player (at 17 years, 111 days) in February 2003 when he came on as a substitute against Australia.

- The 17-year-old gave a stunning performance for England against Turkey, and followed it up with a vital goal for Everton in their 2-1 win over Newcastle.

- In September 2003 (still aged 17), Wayne scored for England against Macedonia. He was the youngest player ever to have scored for his country.

What a year! Nothing could stop Wayne Rooney's rise to greater stardom now.

Wayne Rooney was now "hot property". Everton knew their star was worth a lot of money. Other football clubs wanted him and were willing to pay huge sums to get him. Even though Wayne's heart had always been with his beloved Everton, he knew he could earn far more money if he moved to another club.

After Wayne scored four goals at the 2004 **UEFA** European Football Championship, his name was all over the sports pages of the newspapers. It was reported that Everton offered him £12,000 a week for three years if he would stay. But Wayne knew that at least two clubs could offer him more. Newcastle United and Manchester United both wanted him. Liverpool had always been Wayne's home, but he would soon have to move away for the sake of his career.

MANCHESTER UNITED

This famous football club, based at the Old Trafford Stadium in Manchester, is one of the most popular in the world, with more than 50 million supporters. In the last 20 years, Manchester United has won more than 19 major **honours**. That's more than any other **Premier League** club. It was the manager Sir Matt Busby who made Manchester United a world famous name in the 1950s and 1960s. It was Sir Alex Ferguson's leadership that made Manchester United so successful during the 1990s and beyond.

In 1968, Manchester United became the first English club to win the European Cup. The team holds the record for the most FA Cup wins, and the club is one of the richest in the world.

After selling David Beckham to Real Madrid in 2003, Manchester United was ready to buy another key player. Wayne Rooney was their man!

Another record

Everton had a problem. The club wanted to keep Wayne Rooney but if they sold him they would receive a great deal of money with which to buy new players. By the summer of 2004, Wayne agreed to move. On 31 August 2004, he signed for Manchester United after a deal worth up to £30 million. This **transfer** made Wayne the most expensive teenager in world football. He was still just 18 years old.

When the Manchester United manager Sir Alex Ferguson signed Wayne Rooney, he said their new player was "the best young player this country has seen for the past 30 years".

Wayne Rooney arrives at Old Trafford.

Some people believe the best football players have to be aggressive or forceful. Aggression makes them want to win. But the trouble with aggression is that it can get out of control. Wayne Rooney was famous for his control of the ball but not the control of his temper. He has had to learn that being a good team player needs self control and teamwork.

Broken bones

All footballers are in danger of getting an injury on the pitch or when training. Wayne had damaged toes that kept him out of the team for weeks at a time. In 2006 he injured his foot and people didn't think he would be able to play against Paraguay in the World Cup. Amazingly, he recovered in record time to play just seven weeks after breaking his fourth **metatarsal**.

Wayne receives treatment after injuring his ankle in a UEFA Euro 2004 match against Portugal.

Metatarsals are the five long bones in the foot that connect the ankle bones to the toe bones. The first is linked to the big toe and the fifth links to the little toe. The five metatarsals spread the weight of the body, and they move position to cope with uneven ground.

Injuries are usually caused by a direct blow to the foot, a twisting injury, or overuse. The only treatment for a broken metatarsal is rest. That means no sport or exercise for four to eight weeks. The patient may have to wear special boots or stiff-soled shoes to protect the injury while it heals.

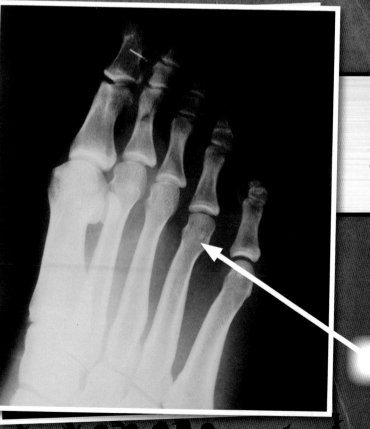

Wayne Rooney broke his fourth metatarsal bone in 2006.

fourth metatarsal

After recovering from his foot injury in 2006, Wayne was selected to play for England in the World Cup. However, during the match in which England lost to Portugal, he again got into trouble. Once more he broke a record, but this time for the wrong reason. He became only the third English player to be given a **red card** while playing a match in the World Cup Finals. Wayne appeared to stamp on the Portuguese player Ricardo Carvalho, right in front of the referee. As play was stopped, another Portuguese player, Cristiano Ronaldo (also one of Wayne's Manchester United teammates), spoke to the referee. Rooney pushed Ronaldo. The referee showed Rooney the red card and he was sent off in the 62nd minute.

2006

Although his performance at the World Cup was poor, 2006 was a good year for Wayne Rooney. He scored two of the goals in a 4–0 victory for Manchester United in the League Cup final against Wigan Athletic. He was also named Man of the Match and awarded his first professional Winners Medal.

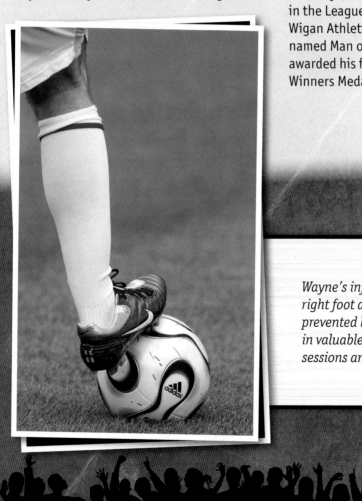

Wayne's injuries to his right foot and ankle prevented him taking part in valuable training sessions and matches.

In October 2006, Wayne captained Manchester United for the first time in a home Champions League match against Copenhagen. This was a week before his 21st birthday, making him one of the youngest captains in the history of the club.

2007

The following year saw more of the "Rooney magic". In the FA Cup tie against Portsmouth, he came on as a **substitute** and scored two goals. One of the goals was an amazing 20-metre chip right over the goalkeeper. Such an impressive shot gave him great headlines once more. Crowds continued to cheer Wayne on as one of the most skilful English players, until he was struck down by another injury. In August 2007 he suffered a hairline fracture to another bone in his foot. The only cure was rest. It was another two months before Wayne was back scoring goals. In his comeback he was the only scorer in a win against Roma. After yet another training injury, this time to his ankle, Wayne was back on the pitch at the end of the year to the delight of his fans and sports writers.

The referee shows Wayne Rooney the red card in the 2006 World Cup match between England and Portugal.

Whether it's Wayne Rooney's performance on the pitch, his foot injuries, or what he does in his private life, he always seems to be in the news. His name sells newspapers and magazines. Reporters and photographers follow him everywhere, and the public want to read about his life.

Wayne gets bad press from time to time, often because of his swearing on the pitch. The English Schools' Football Association (ESFA) once dropped him from making a guest appearance because they thought he was a poor **role model.**

Clean-up

The Football Association is concerned about players using bad language when they are on the pitch. The FA wants to clean up the sport and to set better examples of behaviour. Footballers are role models to thousands of young people, and Wayne is one of the many football stars who can help to make a difference.

Wayne has said that many of the stories about him being "yobbish and always in trouble" aren't true. He says, "In all honesty I try to lead as quiet a life as possible. People close to me will tell you I like a laugh and can be quite sensitive too."

"What's happened to me, all the fame and that, makes no difference. It's up to me to keep my feet on the ground. I've matured a lot." On his website, Wayne puts his success down to "hard work, natural ability, and a certain amount of luck".

People often ask if Wayne has any lucky charms or pre-match dressing room **superstitions.** He says he just has a special routine for getting dressed for a game. He always puts on his shirt sitting at one place, then his socks and boots elsewhere. It seems to work!

Wayne has had to get used to meeting fans and being photographed all the time.

The wages paid to top footballers are beyond most people's wildest dreams. But **Premier League** players don't just earn money from their club. They are paid thousands of pounds by **sponsors** and for appearing at all sorts of public events. Newspapers estimate that Wayne earns £50,000 a week playing for Manchester United and several million a year from sponsorship deals. His main sponsorship contracts are thought to be worth more than £30 million.

Top footballers often spend their money on luxury cars.

Wayne reportedly sold his life story for £5 million. He signed a deal for a five-volume autobiography, to be published over a period of twelve years. His publisher said: "As a footballer, Wayne Rooney has broken records. I think this book deal probably breaks another. I can't think of any book deal like it."

By publishing his own books, Wayne is keen to tell his own story. He said, "I think it will be good for people to see the other side of me and hear things from me for once. I'm just a normal young lad who plays football."

The first volume of Wayne's autobiography came out in July 2006, and was a best-seller.

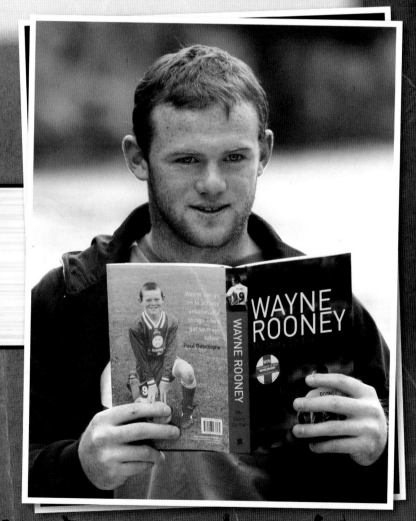

One of the problems with being so rich and famous is that many stories are printed about Wayne's personal life. That means friends and family are also put in the spotlight. Wayne Rooney became famous almost as much for his girlfriend as he did for his football achievements. Wayne met Coleen, who is six months younger than him, when she was 12 and they both lived in Croxteth.

The story goes that on their first date, Wayne took Coleen to the cinema to see *Austin Powers: International Man of Mystery*. It was reported that Wayne proposed to his childhood sweetheart on the forecourt of a garage when she was 17. He apparently gave her a £46,500 diamond engagement ring. The couple now live in a £3.5 million mansion with a pink-tiled swimming pool, a cinema, gym, and games room.

Magazines

Being famous means magazines want to write stories about you, both good and bad. There have been some unkind stories written about Wayne and Coleen, but the couple have also used magazines to help their careers and make even more money. For example, they sold photographs of Coleen's 21st birthday party in 2007 to a celebrity magazine.

WAYNE'S WORLD

Hobbies:	TV, music, video games, films, pool, darts, and relaxing
Favourite TV series:	*Only Fools and Horses*, *Coronation Street*, *EastEnders*
Favourite film:	*Grease*
Favourite video game:	FIFA 07, which he plays with Manchester United teammates Wes Brown, John O'Shea, and Rio Ferdinand.
Favourite music:	Wayne says, "My taste is wide and varied, everything from Damien Rice to 50 Cent. I can sing every tune from the musical *Oliver!*"

Coleen has her own successful career as a model.

Coleen had a small part in the television programme *Hollyoaks* after she left school, but the **media** interest in Wayne has also made her a celebrity.

In 2004 Coleen launched the countdown to the national Jeans for Genes Day to mark the appeal's 10th birthday. This charity supports people with Rett syndrome, which is a development disorder affecting mainly girls. Coleen's younger sister Rosie has Rett syndrome.

Many sports stars have used their name for good causes and Wayne Rooney is one of them. Not only is he a **patron** for a children's **hospice**, but he also supports Manchester United's charity programme. The football club supports the charity **UNICEF** by raising money for Sport for Development. This work uses sport to promote the healthy development of children, and also teaches children about respect, leadership, cooperation, and equality. The "United for UNICEF" partnership has helped around 1.5 million children by raising more than £1.5 million.

Wayne explained how he got involved with the world's largest orphan charity, "**FIFA** for SOS Children's Charity asked me if I would get involved. The work they do is for kids who have suffered and have no families to help them. I know how much it means to have a family that supports you, so I am delighted I can give my support to these kids."

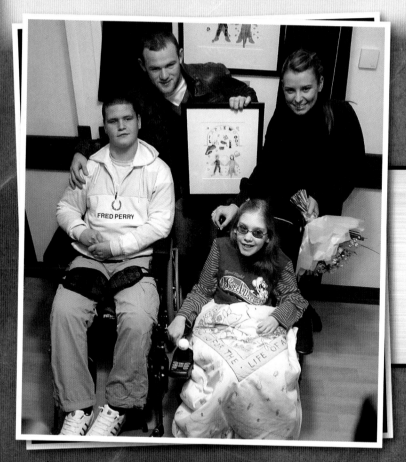

Wayne and Coleen visit children at Alder Hey Children's Hospital in Liverpool. Wayne opened a new unit for children with brain illnesses.

Wayne's football tips

Another of the ways many sports stars try to help others is by coaching young players and giving tips.

Wayne Rooney training at the England camp near Baden-Baden, Germany.

WAYNE'S FIVE-A-SIDE TRICKS

The switch-and-pass
Wayne often demonstrates his trick of running forwards with the ball with a defender by his side, before turning in a tight circle in the opposite direction. If a defender is coming up fast on his left, he turns sharply to the right. The defender will try to follow by going around his back, which allows a few seconds to shoot or pass to another player.

Fooling the goalie
Wayne's tip for scoring is to break away with the ball, turn to the far side of the goal just for an instant, and then turn back and shoot. This will turn the keeper around, opening up the goal for a clearer shot. See if it works!

The challenge for all sports stars is to stay at the top of their game. That means developing further skills, training hard, and keeping fit. In Wayne's case, it also means scoring more goals and trying to beat records. Although he signed to stay with Manchester United for some years, will he one day be tempted to play football abroad? His reply to that question has usually been "I think my game is best suited to England."

Wayne has said: "I love playing football but I think I am like everyone else, I hate losing and love winning. And if the time comes when I am not disappointed when things are definitely not going right, then that's when people should worry."

Alexander Anyukov of Russia and Wayne Rooney fight for the ball during England's Euro 2008 group E qualifying match in Moscow, Russia (Russia won 2-1).

Journalists tried to guess when Wayne and Coleen would get married.

Personal and professional challenges

Wayne and Coleen signed a record-breaking deal with leading celebrity magazine *OK!*, which granted the magazine exclusive rights to cover their wedding. This deal was more than the amount previously paid by magazines for any other celebrity event and reflected their power to appeal to huge audiences.

On a professional level, the big question remaining is: "How long will Wayne Rooney be one of the most exciting players in the game?" It was Bill Kenwright, the chairman of Everton, who once said that Wayne was the greatest player around: "I did a radio interview yesterday and I tried to play down Rooney, but you can't play down Rooney. How can you play down the greatest thing around in football?"

1985	Wayne is born on 24th October in Croxteth, Liverpool.
1994	Wayne joins Everton's Football Youth **Academy**.
2002	Wayne scores his first goal in England's **Premier League** (aged 16).
2002	Wayne wins BBC Young Sports Personality of the Year.
2003	Wayne becomes a fully signed up **professional** player for Everton.
2003	At 17, Wayne becomes the youngest person ever to play for the English national team.
2003	Wayne scores against Macedonia and becomes the youngest player to have scored for England.
2004	Wayne signs for Manchester United.
2005	Wayne wins FIFPro World Young Player of the Year.
2006	Wayne wins PFA Fans' Player of the Year (Premier League).
2006	Wayne publishes the first volume of his **autobiography**.
2007	Wayne and Manchester United win the Premier League.
2008	Wayne and Manchester United win the Premier League and the Champions League. Wayne and Coleen got married on 12th June.

Wayne travels about 12 kilometres (7.5 miles) during a football match.

 During a match, on average Wayne walks for 4,000 metres (13,000 feet), jogs for 4,800 metres (16,000 feet), runs for 1,500 metres (5,000 feet), light sprints for 1,000 metres (3,000 feet), and sprints for 500 metres (1,600 feet).

 In an average game, Wayne heads the ball twice, uses his chest 13 times, and touches the ball with his feet 90 times.

 Team honours:
With Manchester United (2004–present)
• Premier League Champions: 2006–2007, 2007–2008
• Champions League winners: 2008
• Football League Cup winners: 2006
• Community Shield winners: 2007

 Personal honours:
• Barclays Player of the Month: February 2005, December 2005, March 2006
• PFA Team of the Year: 2005–2006
• Sir Matt Busby Player of the Year: 2005–2006
• FIFPro Young Player of the Year: 2005
• PFA Young Player of the Year: 2005, 2006
• PFA Fans' Player of the Year (Premier League): 2006
• BBC's *Match of the Day* Goal of the Season: 2004–2005, 2006–2007

academy school for special training. Football academies are places where football skills are taught.

autobiography person's life story told by that person

debut first public appearance, for example in a sport

FIFA Fédération Internationale de Football Association. FIFA is responsible for organising football's major international tournaments.

honours awards or trophies won by a person or team

hospice special home or hospital providing care for very sick people

mascot something or someone thought to bring good luck to a team

media television, radio, magazines, and newspapers

metatarsal bone of the foot between the ankle and the toes

motto short saying to express an aim or ideal

patron someone who supports an event or a cause

Premier League top level of the English professional football league system

professional someone who gets paid to play their sport

red card card shown by the referee when a player is sent off the pitch for bad behaviour. It can either be handed out to a player who has two yellow cards, or immediately for a more serious offence.

role model successful person whose behaviour is imitated (copied) by others, especially young people

scholarship help in the form of money for pupils to allow them to continue learning. Scholarships can be given to reward sporting achievements.

sponsor company that pays money to a sportsperson in return for advertising their product

substitute reserve football player brought on to the pitch to take over from another player

superstition believing that certain actions can bring good or bad luck

talent scout someone from a football club who goes out and searches for new, talented young players

transfer when a player moves from one football club to another

UEFA Union of European Football Associations

UNICEF United Nations Children's Fund. This charity provides emergency food and healthcare to disadvantaged children.

Books

Essential Sports: Football, Andy Smith (Heinemann Library, 2004)

The Making of a Champion: An International Soccer Star, Ben Godsall (Heinemann Library, 2005)

The Rooney Annual, Wayne Rooney (HarperSport)

Wayne Rooney: My Story So Far, Wayne Rooney (HarperSport, 2006)

Websites

http://www.waynerooney.com
Visit the official Wayne Rooney website and keep up-to-date with all his latest news.

http://www.manutd.com
Learn more about the famous club that Wayne Rooney plays for.

http://www.thefa.com
Find out everything you need to know about the FA and English football.

http://www.thefa.com/GrassrootsNew/News/GetIntoFootball
This part of the FA site has information to help people "Get into football".

http://news.bbc.co.uk/sport
Keep up with all the latest news in the world of football by clicking on the "Football" link of the BBC's sport homepage.

Disclaimer
All the Internet addresses (URLs) given in this book were valid at the time of going to press. However, due to the dynamic nature of the Internet, some addresses may have changed, or sites may have changed or ceased to exist since publication. While the author and Publishers regret any inconvenience this may cause readers, no responsibility for any such changes can be accepted by either the author or the Publishers. It is recommended that adults supervise children on the Internet.